Sushi

AUTHOR: MARLISA SZWILLUS | PHOTOS: TANJA & HARRY BISCHOF

Practical Tips

4   Sushi — An International Favorite
6   Typical Sushi Ingredients
8   Basic Recipe: Sushi Rice
9   Tools for Stirring, Rolling, and Cutting:
    Specialized Utensils
64 Everything Else You Need to Know
65 Putting Together a Sushi Meal:
    Sushi Menus for Company

Inside back cover flap:
    Eating with Chopsticks

Appendix

Inside front flap:
    10 Tips for Success
60 Index
62 Credits

Recipes

10 Sushi Rolls

10 Marinated Tuna Hosomaki	16 Mushroom and Arugula Futomaki
12 Crispy Salmon and Avocado Hosomaki	18 Surimi Uramaki
14 Carrot and Zucchini Hosomaki	20 Shrimp Salad Gunkan-Maki

22 Handmade Sushi

22 Salmon and Roe Nigiri	28 Tofu Temaki
24 Tuna Nigiri	30 Mushroom Temaki
26 Marinated Mackerel Nigiri	30 Steak Temaki
28 Gravlax Temaki	32 Two Types of Temari Sushi

34 Pressed and Freestyle Sushi

34 Pressed Sea Bass and Steelhead Trout Sushi	42 Herring Futomaki
36 Pressed Marinated Sardine Sushi	44 Three Sushi Canapés
38 Pressed Striped Sushi	45 Roast Beef Nigiri
40 Italian-Style Hosomaki	45 Parma Ham Nigiri
40 Asparagus Maki	46 Duck Temaki
42 Vegetable Futomaki	46 Chicken Temaki

48 Sushi Sides

48 Spinach Salad with Sesame Seed Dressing	53 Egg Flower Soup
50 Vegetables with Teriyaki Dip	53 Tofu Miso Soup
50 Radish Carrot Salad	54 Vegetable Shrimp Tempura
51 Chinese Cabbage Rolls	56 Beef Tenderloin Skewers
51 Sprout Salad	56 Chicken Yakitori
52 Chicken and Glass Noodle Soup	58 Coconut-Lime Ice Cream
	58 Tropical Fruit Salad

Sushi—An International Favorite

Sushi is the perfect way to make a big impression with something small.
And best of all, it is easy to make!

Westerners are crazier than ever about these Japanese appetizers. As sophisticated delicacies, they're a culinary marvel and a beauty to behold. They originated from the idea that fresh fish could be preserved on rice mixed with vinegar. Over the centuries, this method of preparation has spawned myriad variations.

Easy to make yourself

Eating sushi in a restaurant or bar is a costly pleasure. That's why more and more sushi fans are making their own. The same sushi that professional sushi chefs throw together in a flash will take a little longer for amateurs, but with a bit of practice, home cooks can make it look just as good. These little delicacies taste especially good when homemade, and they really make an impression.

With or without raw fish

A growing number of adventurous consumers are overcoming their aversion to raw fish and discovering a whole new world of enjoyment. In addition to fresh, tender fish, other delicious ingredients can be used both in the sushi and on the side, including vegetables, herbs, and cheese, and cooked ingredients such as shrimp, omelets, and even meat and poultry. It all depends on what you like. There's all kinds of room for individual creativity.

Absolutely essential: vinegar water

Sushi preparation should always involve a small bowl of water with a dash of rice vinegar. While shaping sushi, moisten your hands frequently with vinegar water so that the rice doesn't stick anywhere you don't want it to. Vinegar water's anti-sticking effect is also helpful when cutting maki rolls and shaping sushi in molds. Always be sure to wipe the knife or mold with a cloth moistened with vinegar water.

Favorite sushi shapes

Nigiri, the original form of sushi, started with raw fish on top, a rectangular block of rice on the bottom, and with just a trace of wasabi paste in between. Today, toppings vary widely. Maki, rolled with the help of a bamboo mat, is constructed using nori sheets outside and rice inside, plus a seasoned filling. Thin rolls are called hosomaki and thick rolls are futomaki. Inside-out sushi, in which the positions of the rice and nori sheet are reversed, is known as uramaki. For gunkan-maki, the rice ball is surrounded by a strip of nori. Gunkan-maki always has a soft filling. With temaki, rice and all sorts of ingredients are enclosed in a crispy nori-sheet "bag."

How to eat sushi

Along with the sushi, each person receives a small bowl of soy sauce into which a little (!) wasabi, that blazing hot green horseradish paste, is stirred. Sushi can be eaten with chopsticks, but it isn't mandatory. True sushi connoisseurs eat sushi with their fingers. In any case, knives and forks are strictly taboo! From time to time, eat a small piece of pickled ginger or drink some tea to cleanse your palate. Sushi is generally eaten whole. Only temaki in a bag requires several bites.

Measurement guide

One maki or two gunkan-maki rolls are enough for one person as a snack or appetizer. As a full meal, serve two or three times that amount, depending on your appetite and whether you're serving any other type of sushi. For nigiri served as an appetizer or snack, count on two per person; as a meal, you'll need from eight to ten, provided you're not serving any other sushi type.

Eating sushi without set rules

Unlike Westerners, the Japanese don't hold to a fixed sequence of courses for their meals, so there really isn't any set sushi menu. Eat them in whatever order you want. In addition to an assortment of different sushi varieties, you can serve soup, salad, pickled vegetables, small meat skewers, and more sushi. (Recipes for dishes to serve before, during, and after can be found starting on page 48.) All dishes are placed on the table at the same time, followed only by fruit or ice cream. If you're having maki or temaki sushi, it's best to eat them first because the moisture in the rice and filling quickly renders the crispy nori leaves soft and then soggy.

Three beverages go with sushi

Traditionally, sushi is accompanied by green tea, but sake (Japanese rice wine) is also in keeping with proper style. It is heated by placing the container in hot water and then drunk from tiny porcelain cups. Another drink that goes well with sushi is a light-colored beer, whether Japanese or not.

Ideal for any occasion

Whether you eat it with chopsticks or your fingers, sushi isn't just the ideal snack for between meals: it's also excellent as a light and healthy lunch or dinner. These delicious bites serve as an extra-special treat when you're entertaining guests and want to surprise them.

Pure fish

Finger food

Sake, etc.

Typical Ingredients

When you use fresh, authentic ingredients, your sushi is virtually guaranteed to come out perfectly, no matter what type you try!

Ingredients are especially important with sushi. You don't want to hide or distort the fine flavor of fish, vegetables, eggs, etc. We recommend the use of Japanese products, because their flavor is much more delicate than that of comparable products from other Asian countries. All ingredients are available in the Asian section of large supermarkets and, certainly, in Asian markets.

Sushi rice is special, polished, round-grain rice that is grainy and slightly sticky after cooking (which it has to be in order to be shaped). In a pinch, you can use Italian round-grain risotto. Non-sticky rice is unsuitable for sushi, as is aromatic long-grain or basmati rice.

Rice vinegar is derived from rice wine in the traditional manner. It comes in both light and dark versions. The light, straw-colored variety has a mild, sweetish aroma and is much mellower than Western vinegars. As a seasoning, rice vinegar is what gives sushi rice its slightly acidic flavor. However, you can also use fruit vinegar mixed with a little water.

Nori sheets are made of dried, pressed seaweed. The dark-green, paper-thin sheets are an important ingredient for enclosing maki and temaki sushi. Toasted nori sheets are more flavorful than untoasted.

Mirin is a sweet, highly alcoholic Japanese rice wine that's used exclusively for cooking. Amontillado sherry can be substituted.

Wasabi is Japanese green horseradish and is an essential part of sushi cuisine. Wasabi comes in a paste or as a powder that's stirred into liquid. But watch out! It's extremely hot and will bring tears to your eyes.

Japanese soy sauce (shoyu) is a dark sauce that is a must for eating sushi! It is brewed naturally in the traditional manner using soybeans, wheat, water, and salt. What distinguishes it from chemically produced soy sauce is its transparency and tangy aroma. Light soy sauce enhances the flavors of the other ingredients.

Pickled ginger (gari-shoga) consists of paper-thin slices of ginger marinated in sake (rice wine), mirin, or sugar and salt. Once opened, commercial ginger keeps for months in the refrigerator.

Instant dashi is a basic Japanese soup powder made from kelp and dried fish that is added to liquid.

Sesame oil in its dark version is made from toasted sesame seeds and used sparingly (usually just a drop or teaspoonful at a time) as a highly flavorful seasoning. Light sesame oil, which is made from untoasted sesame seeds, has a neutral flavor and is used for frying.

shi rice

Rice vinegar

Nori sheets

Mirin

Wasabi

Soy sauce

ckled ginger

Instant dashi

Sesame oil

Sushi Rice

You can vary the combination of seasonings as desired,
but you must include vinegar, sugar, and salt!

9 oz (250 g) sushi rice
1 small piece kombu (dried kelp: about
   2 in x 2 in (5 x 5 cm)) (as desired)
2 tbs light rice vinegar
2 tsp mirin
2 tsp sugar
½ tsp salt

For 2 batches rolled or handmade sushi, or
1 batch pressed sushi.
◎ Prep time: 50 minutes
Per sushi approx.: 970 calories, 18 g protein,
0 g fat, 213 g carbohydrates

1 Put rice in a strainer and rinse under running
water until water runs clear. Drain.

2 In a pot, combine 1¼–1⅔ cups (300–400 ml)
water (depending on package instructions) and
kombu and bring to a boil. Boil uncovered for

2 minutes, then cover and simmer over low heat
for about 15 minutes.

3 Remove pot from heat, take off lid and cover
rice with a kitchen towel. Let stand for 10 minutes.
Stir together rice vinegar, mirin, sugar, and salt
until the mixture is clear.

4 Transfer to a large, shallow bowl. Remove and
discard kombu. Carefully cut and fold sushi rice
with a broad wooden rice paddle while drizzling
with rice vinegar mixture.

5 Use rice paddle to turn and toss rice so it cools
faster. Don't stir or mash the grains. At the same
time, blow air on rice with a fan (or hairdryer set
to blow cool air) for 10 minutes. Cover finished
rice with a damp kitchen towel and use when it
reaches room temperature.

Specialized Utensils

The right utensils always do the job faster and easier.

As a matter of fact, preparing sushi with authentic utensils is also a lot more fun. If you want to have the real experience, go to a Japanese shop, a household supply store, or relevant section of a department store.

1   A flat, unvarnished wooden tub (hangiri) is ideal for cooling rice because the wood absorbs the excess moisture. You can also use an unglazed earthenware bowl, or any other kind of bowl.

2   A broad, wooden rice paddle is good for working the vinegar mixture into the rice. You can also use the paddle to fan the rice so it cools.

3   Fish bone tweezers with wide, flat grips allow you to safely extract fish bones without breaking them off.

4   Knives must have heavy, super-sharp blades. You'll need one knife with a long, narrow blade for cutting fish into thin, even slices, preferably a special sushi or sashimi knife. You'll also need a utility knife for chopping vegetables and other ingredients. For guaranteed sharpness, use a ceramic whetstone or sharpening steel.

5   It's very important to have a stable board for cutting, whether it's made of natural wood, ceramic, or glass. Be sure to scrub the board thoroughly after every use. Glass or porcelain boards can be washed in the dishwasher.

6   A bamboo sushi mat (makisu) is a useful tool for shaping all kinds of maki sushi—including hosomaki, futomaki, and uramaki—into perfect, decorative rolls. Clean the mat thoroughly after each use.

Sushi utensils, left to right: Wooden cutting board, knives, fish bone tweezers, rolling mats, and wooden paddle

Sushi Rolls

I can never get enough of my favorite maki! The contrast between marinated tuna, juicy rice, and the crisp seaweed wrapper is truly inspired. Plus, there's that little hint of spiciness—absolute perfection!

Marinated Tuna Hosomaki

For the sushi
4½ oz (125 g) fresh tuna fillet
2 tsp mayonnaise
1 tsp dark sesame oil
1 tsp rice vinegar
¼ tsp shichimi togarashi
  (hot seasoning mix)
2 sheets toasted nori
½ recipe prepared sushi rice (see page 8)
Vinegar water
For the garnish
Shichimi togarashi (hot seasoning mix)
Some chopped chives

Makes 24 sushi | ◉ Prep time: 30 minutes
Per sushi approx.: 35 calories, 1 g protein,
1 g fat, 4 g carbohydrates

1 Pat tuna dry and cut into strips ½ inch (1 cm) wide. Combine mayonnaise, sesame oil, vinegar, and shichimi togarashi. Dredge fish strips in this mixture, cover, and marinate for 5 minutes. In the meantime, cut nori sheets in half crosswise.

2 Using a bamboo rolling mat, make four maki rolls from the prepared rice and marinated tuna (see pages 12–13). Moisten the blade of a knife with vinegar water and cut each roll into six equal-sized pieces. Arrange with cut sides up. Serve sprinkled with a little shichimi togarashi and some chopped chives.

classic

Crispy Salmon and Avocado Hosomaki

One of countless sushi varieties, it begs to be sampled, then leaves you intrigued to try all the others.

9 oz (250 g) fresh salmon fillet with skin | 1 tbs potato or wheat flour | 2 tbs oil | 2 sheets toasted nori | ¼ ripe avocado | 2 tsp lemon juice | ½ recipe prepared sushi rice (see page 8) | 1 scant tsp wasabi paste | Vinegar water

Makes 24 sushi | ⊚ Prep time: 40 minutes
Per sushi approx.: 55 calories, 3 g protein, 3 g fat, 5 g carbohydrates

1 Pat salmon dry and dust lightly with flour. In a nonstick pan, heat oil and sauté with skin side down for 2 minutes until crispy. Remove from pan and dab off fat. Cut lengthwise into strips.

2 Cut nori sheets in half crosswise. Peel avocado, cut into 8 wedges, and immediately brush with lemon juice.

3 Place half a nori sheet on a bamboo mat, shiny side down, so that the long edge is flush with the bottom of the mat (Figure 1). Moisten your hands with vinegar water.

4 Cover nori sheet with a ¼ in–½ in (½–1 cm) layer of room-temperature sushi rice, leaving ¾ in (2 cm) uncovered at the two longer edges. Make a lengthwise depression in the rice and brush a little wasabi paste into the depression with your fingertip (Figure 2).

5 Place one quarter of salmon and avocado strips into the depression, arranging them tightly together (Figure 3). Lift up edge of bamboo mat closest to you and use it to wrap the nori sheet and rice around filling to form a tight roll while holding filling in place with your hands so that it remains in the center. Just before the roll is complete, lift up the end of the mat and roll a little further so that it doesn't get caught in the roll.

6 Now the sushi roll takes on its final shape. Place part of the bamboo mat on top of the roll and carefully but firmly press it together with both hands (Figure 4). Depending on the way you exert pressure, maki sushi will be round or square. Remove the bamboo mat. Follow the same procedure to make three more rolls.

7 Place sushi roll on a board, seam-side down. Firmly press in on the open ends with your fingers. Moisten a sharp knife with vinegar water and cut roll in half crosswise.

8 Place halves side by side and cut into thirds. Slice rolls either straight across or at an angle. Each roll makes 6 small morsels. Arrange sushi cut sides up (Figure 5). Serve with Japanese soy sauce, wasabi paste, and pickled ginger.

few ingredients | lots of flavor

Carrot and Zucchini Hosomaki

This is how to make sushi that's especially beautiful: with carrots and zucchini cut into thick sticks that are precise and uniform.

1 large carrot | 1 piece firm zucchini (about 4 in (10 cm) long) | 2 tbs sake (Japanese rice wine) | ½ tsp sugar | ¼ tsp salt | 2 sheets toasted nori | ½ recipe prepared sushi rice (page 8) | 1 scant tsp wasabi paste | Vinegar water

Makes 24 sushi | ⏲ Prep time: 40 minutes
Per sushi approx.: 25 calories, 0 g protein, 1 g fat, 5 g carbohydrates

1   Clean and peel carrots. First cut lengthwise into slices ¼ in (½ cm) thick and then cut into sticks ¼ in (½ cm) thick. Clean zucchini, rinse, and dry. Using a long knife, first cut off a ¼ in (½ cm) thick strip of peel, including flesh, then cut crosswise into sticks ¼ in (½ cm) thick.

2   In a small pan, combine rice wine, sugar, salt, and 2½ teaspoons water and bring to a boil. Add carrot sticks, cover, and simmer for 1 minute. Remove from heat, add zucchini strips, and let cool in the liquid. Remove vegetables, drain, and pat dry.

3   Cut nori sheets in half crosswise. Moisten your hands with vinegar water. With the help of a rolling mat (see pages 12–13), make four maki rolls using the prepared rice, wasabi paste, and marinated vegetables. Moisten a knife with vinegar water.

Cut rolls into six pieces and arrange decoratively. Serve with Japanese soy sauce, wasabi paste, and pickled ginger.

VARIATION – CUCUMBER AND SESAME SEED HOSOMAKI

In a small, ungreased pan, toast 1 tablespoon white sesame seeds over medium heat while stirring until golden brown. Remove from pan and let cool on a small plate. In the meantime, rinse 1 piece pickling or slicing cucumber (about 4 in (10 cm) long) and dry. Using a long knife, first cut off a ¼ in (½ cm) thick strip of peel, including flesh, then cut crosswise into strips ¼ in (½ cm) thick. Cut 2 sheets toasted nori in half crosswise. Moisten your hands with vinegar water. With the help of a rolling mat (see pages 12–13), make four maki rolls using ½ recipe prepared sushi rice (see page 8), 1¼ teaspoons wasabi paste, cucumber strips, and toasted sesame seeds. Moisten a knife with vinegar water. Cut rolls into six equal-sized pieces and serve cut side up.

TIP—CLEVERLY MADE

Instead of using your hands, distribute rice loosely over the half sheets of nori with a tablespoon dipped in vinegar water. Proceed carefully to avoid mashing the rice, and dip spoon in vinegar water at frequent intervals.

left: Cucumber and Sesame Seed Hosomaki | right: Carrot and Zucchini Hosomaki

versatile filling

Mushroom and Arugula Futomaki

Thick maki rolls like these are made from a whole nori sheet with at least three ingredients in the filling.

4 dried shiitake mushrooms | 2 tsp sugar | 2 tbs light soy sauce | 4 tsp mirin | 2 oz (50 g) arugula | 2½ oz (80 g) omelet (page 26) | 2 sheets toasted nori | ½ recipe prepared sushi rice (page 8) | 1 scant tsp wasabi paste | Vinegar water

Makes 16 sushi | ⦾ Prep time: 25 minutes | Soaking time: 20 minutes
Per sushi approx.: 45 calories, 1 g protein, 1 g fat, 8 g carbohydrates

1 Pour ⅔ cup (150 ml) boiling water over dried mushrooms and let soak for 20 minutes. Remove from water, rinse thoroughly, and remove hard stems. Pour soaking water through a fine strainer and pour into a small saucepan.

2 Add mushroom caps, sugar, soy sauce, and mirin to the saucepan and simmer for 10 minutes. Pour off water and drain. Cut mushrooms into strips. Rinse arugula, pat dry, remove hard stems, and chop leaves coarsely. Cut omelet into strips.

3 Using a rolling mat, make two thick maki sushi rolls (see pages 12–13). For each roll, place 1 sheet nori on rolling mat. Moisten your hands with vinegar water. Distribute half the rice over the nori sheet, leaving ¾ in (2 cm) uncovered at the two longer edges.

4 Spread ½ teaspoon wasabi on top. Lay half prepared ingredients crosswise on rice and shape it all into a thick roll. Make a second roll from remaining ingredients. Moisten a sharp knife with vinegar water. Cut each futomaki roll into eight equal-sized pieces.

VARIATION—TROUT FUTOMAKI
Rinse 8 small green lettuce leaves, pat dry, and remove thick ribs. Rinse 4 sprigs dill and pat dry. Cut 7 oz (200 g) smoked, skinless trout fillet lengthwise into strips about ½ in (1 cm) wide. Moisten your hands with vinegar water. Using a rolling mat, make two thick maki rolls (see previous recipe) using 2 sheets toasted nori, a half recipe sushi rice (see page 8), 1 scant teaspoon wasabi paste, lettuce leaves, dill, and trout fillet, allowing lettuce to protrude slightly at both ends of the nori. Cut each roll into eight equal-sized pieces.

VARIATION—SQUASH FUTOMAKI
Rinse 1 small box garden cress, shake dry, and remove leaves. Rinse 1 piece cucumber (4 in (10 cm) long) and dry. Using a long knife, first cut off a ¼ in (½ cm) thick strip of peel, including flesh, then cut crosswise into sticks ¼ in (½ cm) thick. Drain 5 oz (150 g) pickled squash and cut into pencil-thin strips. Make two thick maki rolls using 2 toasted nori sheets, ½ recipe prepared sushi rice (page 8), 1 scant teaspoon wasabi paste, cucumber, squash, and cress. Cut each roll into eight pieces.

favorite inside-out roll

Surimi Uramaki

This sushi is also known worldwide as "California Rolls" and was supposedly created on North America's West Coast.

2 tbs white sesame seeds + a few black sesame seeds (optional) | 4 surimi (imitation crab) sticks (about 2 oz (60 g)) | ¼ ripe avocado | 2 tsp lemon juice | 1 piece cucumber (about 4 in (10 cm) long) | 2 sheets toasted nori | ½ recipe prepared sushi rice (page 8) | 1½ tsp mayonnaise | 1 tsp soy sauce | Vinegar water

Makes 16 sushi | ⊚ Prep time: 40 minutes
Per sushi approx.: 60 calories, 2 g protein,
3 g fat, 7 g carbohydrates

1 In an ungreased pan, toast white sesame seeds until golden brown. Remove from pan and let cool. If desired, mix with black sesame seeds. Pat crab sticks dry and cut in half lengthwise. Peel avocado, cut lengthwise into strips, and immediately drizzle with lemon juice.

2 Rinse cucumber and dry. Using a long knife, first cut a ¼ in (½ cm) thick strip of peel, including flesh, then cut crosswise into sticks ¼ in (½ cm) thick.

3 Wrap two bamboo rolling mats in plastic wrap. Place 1 sheet nori on a bamboo mat with shiny side down so that the long edge is flush with the bottom of the mat. Moisten your hands with vinegar water. Distribute half the sushi rice on nori sheet, leaving ¾ in (2 cm) uncovered at the two longer edges. Gently press down on rice. Place the other mat on top, turn it over and remove top mat. The nori is now on top.

4 Stir together mayonnaise and soy sauce. Spread across lower third of the nori sheet. Top with half crab sticks, cucumber strips, and avocado strips. Using a rolling mat, make a tight roll (as for futomaki, page 16) using rice, nori, and filling. If desired, make it slightly square. Repeat process with remaining ingredients to make a second roll.

5 Moisten a sharp knife with vinegar water. Cut each sushi roll into eight equal-sized pieces. Roll each sushi in toasted sesame seeds halfway around its circumference. Serve cut side up.

VARIATION—TUNA URAMAKI
For the filling, cut 1 large carrot lengthwise into thin sticks and blanch. Blanch 3 oz (100 g) spinach in salted water, plunge into cold water and pull apart. Cut 3 oz (100 g) very fresh tuna fillet into pencil-thin strips and marinate in a little mirin. Make four rolls as described in the recipe, but with halved nori sheets. If desired, roll sushi in 3 tablespoons flying fish roe.

for company | easy

Shrimp Salad Gunkan-Maki

This sushi is designed for soft fillings. If you're feeling brave, try inventing your own!

1 piece fresh ginger (¾ in (2 cm)) | 6–8 sprigs Italian parsley | 5 oz (150 g) cooked, peeled shrimp | ⅓ cup (80 ml) crème fraîche | 2 tsp lime or lemon juice | 2 sheets toasted nori | ½ recipe prepared sushi rice (page 8) | Sea salt | Freshly ground pepper | Vinegar water

Makes 12 sushi | ⓘ Prep time: 30 minutes
Per sushi approx.: 60 calories, 3 g protein, 1 g fat, 9 g carbohydrates

1 Peel ginger and grate very finely. Rinse parsley, shake dry, and remove coarse stems. Set aside 1 tablespoon leaves for garnish and finely chop the rest. Rinse shrimp and pat dry.

2 Stir together crème fraîche, ginger, and lime or lemon juice until smooth. Add chopped parsley and shrimp. Season shrimp salad to taste with salt and pepper.

3 Trim any frayed edges from nori sheets. Cut nori sheets lengthwise into 12 strips about 1¼ in (3 cm) wide and 6 in (15 cm) long.

4 Moisten your hands with vinegar water. Shape prepared sushi rice into 12 rectangular blocks. Wrap a nori strip around each block of rice, shiny side out. Place 1 or 2 mashed grains of rice under the end of the strip and press onto the nori.

5 Gently press rice down inside the nori sheet. Distribute shrimp salad evenly on top. Cut parsley leaves into fine strips and use as garnish.

VARIATION—ROE DUNKAN-MAKI

Trim 2 sheets toasted nori as described in the recipe on the left. Moisten your hands with vinegar water. Shape ½ recipe prepared sushi rice (see page 8) into 12 rectangular blocks. Wrap a nori strip around each block of rice and secure it with rice grains. Cut 6 thin cucumber slices in half. Cut each slice to form a fan and use to garnish sushi.

VARIATION—SCRAMBLED EGG GUNKAN-MAKI

Trim 2 sheets toasted nori as described in the recipe on the left. Beat 3 eggs, 1¼ teaspoons light soy sauce, 2 teaspoons mirin, and 1 pinch salt. Heat 1¼ teaspoons dark sesame oil, add eggs, sprinkle with chopped chives, and cook until firm, stirring occasionally. Moisten your hands with vinegar water. Shape ½ recipe of prepared sushi rice (see page 8) into 12 rectangular blocks. Wrap a nori strip around each block of rice and secure with rice grains. Gently press rice down into the nori sheet. Fill sushi with scrambled egg and sprinkle with chopped chives.

left: Scrambled Egg Gunkan-Maki | middle: Roe Gunkan-Maki | right: Shrimp Salad Gunkan-Maki

Handmade Sushi

Don't they look fantastic? And they taste that way, too! Serve nigiri sushi as an extravagant appetizer, and buy really good salmon to make it. Don't tell anyone, but it's also relatively quick to prepare.

Salmon and Roe Nigiri

5 oz (150 g) fresh salmon fillet (preferably
    center-cut)
1¼ tsp wasabi paste
½ recipe prepared sushi rice (page 8)
2 tsp salmon or trout roe
Vinegar water

Makes 8 sushi | ◎ Prep time: 30 minutes
Per sushi approx.: 100 calories, 5 g protein,
3 g fat, 13 g carbohydrates

1 With a sharp knife, cut salmon fillet across the
grain and at a slight angle into eight thin slices
about 1¼ x 2 in (3 x 5 cm).

2 Spread a thin layer of wasabi on one side of
each piece of salmon. Moisten your hands with
vinegar water. Shape rice into 8 rectangular blocks.

3 One at a time, place salmon slices on the palm
of your left hand, wasabi side up. Place rice block
on top and gently press down. Turn over sushi and
carefully mold it into a uniform shape (see pages
24–25). Garnish with salmon roe and arrange on
plates. Serve with Japanese soy sauce, wasabi
paste, and pickled ginger for dipping and eating.

ALSO DELICIOUS!
Instead of raw salmon, try a layer of smoked salmon
or gravlax.

classic
Tuna Nigiri

This is the original sushi. Comprising rice and raw fish, it's always a favorite of true fans. Here's one of the best recipes!

5 oz (150 g) fresh tuna fillet | 1¼ tsp wasabi paste | ½ recipe prepared sushi rice (page 8) | Vinegar water | For garnish (optional): Chives and 1 egg

Makes 8 sushi | ⊚ Prep time: 30 minutes
Per sushi approx.: 115 calories, 6 g protein, 4 g fat, 13 g carbohydrates

1 With a sharp knife, cut tuna across the grain and at a slight angle into 8 thin, equal-sized slices about 1¼ x 2 in (3 x 5 cm) (Figure 1).

1 Spread a dab of wasabi down the center of each piece of tuna with your fingertip.

2 Moisten your hands with vinegar water. Shape sushi rice into 8 rectangular, relatively loose blocks (Figure 2).

3 One at a time, place tuna slices on the palm of your left hand, wasabi side up. Place rice block on top and press down gently with your thumb and index finger so that the rice and fish stick together (Figure 4).

4 Turn sushi over onto the palm of your other hand. Using your thumb and index finger, gently press the longer edges of the sushi onto the rice and shape the whole thing into a uniform rectangle.

5 Use your index finger to shape the rice side of the sushi to give it the typical nigiri dome shape.

6 Serve sushi "plain" (Figure 5) or garnish as desired. Top each sushi with either 2 chive leaves or several chopped chives. They're also pretty with an "egg yolk pearl." In this case, hard-boil 1 egg, let cool, and peel. With the back of a spoon, press egg yolk through a small fine-mesh strainer. Place the equivalent of one small pearl on top of each sushi. Serve with Japanese soy sauce, wasabi paste, and pickled ginger.

ALSO DELICIOUS!
You can make a diverse range of nigiri sushi based on this recipe. For example, use a raw fillet of saltwater fish such as sole, flounder, sea bass, or mahi-mahi, or fresh-water fish such as trout or char. This nigiri also tastes great with a layer of thinly sliced, semi-cooked scallops and calamari.

sophisticated & spicy

Marinated Mackerel Nigiri

This is for everyone who loves fish, but not when it's raw. Through curing and marinating, it's possible to "cold cook" the mackerel.

6 oz (180 g) fresh mackerel fillet with skin | 4 tsp salt | ¼ cup (50 ml) rice vinegar | 2 tsp mirin | ½ tsp sugar | 1¼ tsp wasabi paste | ½ recipe prepared sushi rice (page 8) | Vinegar water

Makes 8 sushi | ⓘ Prep time: 30 minutes | Marinating time: 5 hours
Per sushi approx.: 110 calories, 5 g protein, 3 g fat, 15 g carbohydrates

1   Rub salt into mackerel, wrap in plastic wrap, and refrigerate for 4 hours. Briefly rinse off salt and pat fish dry. Place in a shallow bowl. Combine vinegar, mirin, and sugar to make a marinade and marinate in refrigerator for 1 hour, turning once.

2   Remove fillet from marinade and pat dry. Detach the skin as follows: Starting at the tail, use a knife to separate a little skin from flesh. Grasp meat with one hand and pull off skin with the other. Cut mackerel at a slight angle into eight equal-sized pieces.

3   Dab wasabi paste onto one side of each fish slice with your fingertips. Moisten your hands with vinegar water. Shape sushi rice into eight rectangular blocks. Make nigiri sushi from fish and rice (see pages 24–25).

GARNISHING TIP

Rinse, clean, and finely chop green part of a green onion. Peel and grate about 1¼ in (3 cm) ginger root. Garnish each sushi with one tiny pearl of green onion and ginger.

VARIATION—OMELET NIGIRI

Mix together ⅓ cup (70 ml) instant dashi (fish stock), 2 teaspoons mirin, 2 teaspoons light soy sauce, 4 teaspoons sugar, 1 pinch salt, and 6 eggs. In a small pan, heat 1 tablespoon oil and cook a thick omelet for 15–20 minutes over very low heat until firm. Let cool and cut into eight 1¼ x 2 in (3 x 5 cm) pieces. As described on pages 24–25, make nigiri sushi using ½ recipe prepared sushi rice (see page 8) and omelet. Secure in the middle with a chive.

VARIATION—SHRIMP NIGIRI

Pierce 8 raw, unpeeled shrimp (about 1 oz (30 g)) with a skewer. Cook in salted water for 3 minutes. Plunge into cold water and remove skewer. Peel shrimp and cut open underside lengthwise but do not cut all the way through. Combine 4 teaspoons rice vinegar, 2 teaspoons lime juice, ¼ cup mirin, and ½ teaspoon sugar and marinate shrimp for 10 minutes. Remove, pat dry, and season underside with a tiny dab of wasabi paste. Make nigiri sushi using ½ recipe prepared sushi rice as described above.

as appetizer | as late-night bite

Gravlax Temaki

Always a hit, whether as an appetizer or snack.

⅔ cup (150 g) zucchini | 5 oz (150 g) piece of gravlax | 3 sheets toasted nori | ½ recipe prepared sushi rice (page 8) | ½ tsp mild mustard | Vinegar water

Makes 6 sushi | ⊙ Prep time: 30 minutes
Per sushi approx.: 135 calories, 7 g protein, 3 g fat, 18 g carbohydrates

1   Rinse zucchini, clean, and pat dry. Cut one-third into thin strips about 4 in (10 cm) long and finely chop the rest. Dice gravlax as finely as possible. Mix diced zucchini and gravlax. Cut nori sheets in half crosswise.

2   Moisten your hands with vinegar water. Shape rice into six balls. Place a ½ sheet nori in the palm of your left hand, shiny side down. Place rice ball in the center and dab on mustard with your fingertip. Place one-sixth of the gravlax and zucchini strips on the rice. Squeeze gently so it all sticks together.

3   Roll nori sheet around filling into a cone. Seal the outside edge of the nori with a couple mashed grains of rice.

VARIATION
Make other delicious fillings by replacing gravlax with smoked salmon, herring fillet, raw salmon fillet, or raw tuna fillet.

for vegetarians | inexpensive

Tofu Temaki

For smaller bites, cut nori sheets into quarters and use ingredients to make 12 temaki.

2 green onions | ½ red bell pepper | 6 small green lettuce leaves | 5 oz (150 g) tofu | 3 sheets toasted nori | ½ recipe prepared sushi rice (page 8) | 1 scant tsp wasabi paste | Vinegar water

Makes 6 sushi | ⊙ Prep time: 30 minutes
Per sushi approx.: 105 calories, 4 g protein, 1 g fat, 19 g carbohydrates

1   Rinse green onions and bell pepper, clean, and cut into thin strips no more than 4 in (10 cm) long. Rinse lettuce and pat dry. Cut tofu into strips no more than 4 in (10 cm) long and the thickness of a finger. Cut nori sheets in half crosswise.

2   Moisten your hands with vinegar water. Shape rice into six balls. Place a ½ sheet nori in the palm of your left hand, shiny side down. Place 1 lettuce leaf and a rice ball in the center and dab on wasabi with your fingertip. Place one-sixth of the prepared ingredients on the rice. Squeeze gently so it all sticks together.

3   Roll nori sheet around filling into a cone so that the filling doesn't fall out. Seal the outside edge of the nori with a couple mashed grains of rice.

left: Tofu Temaki | right: Gravlax Temaki

decorative and really aasy

Mushroom Temaki

Delicious filled cones: Sushi fun for all.

14 oz (400 g) oyster mushrooms | 4 tsp oil | 2 tsp lemon juice | 2–4 tsp light soy sauce | 3 tender stalks celery with leaves | 6 small endive leaves | 3 sheets toasted nori | ½ recipe prepared sushi rice (page 8) | 1 scant tsp wasabi paste | Vinegar water

Makes 6 sushi | ⊚ Prep time: 40 minutes
Per sushi approx.: 145 calories, 4 g protein, 7 g fat, 21 g carbohydrates

1   Clean mushrooms, remove stem ends and hard spots, and cut into strips. In a pan, heat oil and sauté mushrooms while stirring until all liquid has evaporated. Season to taste with lemon juice and soy sauce.

2   Rinse celery, clean, and halve lengthwise and crosswise. Rinse endive leaves and pat dry. Cut nori sheets in half crosswise. Moisten your hands with vinegar water. Shape rice into six balls

3   Place a ½ sheet nori in the palm of your left hand, shiny side down. Place 1 endive leaf and one rice ball in the center and dab on wasabi paste with your fingertip. Place one-sixth of the prepared ingredients on the rice and squeeze gently. Roll up temaki.

Eurasian combination

Steak Temaki

The secret: It's not the quantity but the quality of meat that counts.

1 piece daikon radish (3 oz (100 g)) | 1 small dried chili pepper | 6 oak leaf lettuce leaves | 1 small carrot | 2–4 tsp dark sesame oil | 5 oz (150 g) beefsteak | ½ recipe prepared sushi rice (page 8) | 3 sheets toasted nori | 6 long chive leaves | Sea salt | Vinegar water

Makes 6 sushi | ⊚ Prep time: 40 minutes
Per sushi approx.: 140 calories, 7 g protein, 4 g fat, 19 g carbohydrates

1   Peel radish and grate finely. Crush chili pepper very finely and mix with radish. Rinse lettuce leaves and pat dry. Peel carrot, cut into thin slices lengthwise, and then into very fine strips.

2   In a small pan, heat oil and fry steak on both sides for 2–3 minutes. Remove from pan and dab with paper towels. Salt steak lightly and slice as finely as possible against the grain. Squeeze moisture out of radish-chili pepper mixture and shape into six loosely packed balls.

3   Moisten your hands with vinegar water. Shape rice into six balls. Fill half a nori sheet with a lettuce leaf, rice ball, and a sixth of the carrot strips, steak, and radish-chili pepper mixture. Roll into cone-shaped temaki. Knot chives around the bottom.

left: Mushroom Temaki | right: Steak Temaki

finger food for an asian party

Two Types of Temari Sushi

Anyone can make these! It's easy when you use the eggcup trick. You'll find it under "TIP" following the recipe.

For garnish:
1 egg | 12 small dill tips | 6 Italian parsley leaves | 2 tsp chopped chives
For the sushi:
5 oz (150 g) fresh skinless steelhead trout fillet | 5 oz (150 g) fresh halibut fillet | ½ recipe prepared sushi rice (page 8) | 1 scant tsp wasabi paste | Vinegar water

Makes 12 sushi | ◎ Prep time: 50 minutes
Per sushi approx.: 85 calories, 4 g protein, 9 g fat, 3 g carbohydrates

1 For the garnish, hard-boil egg for about 8 minutes. Plunge into ice-cold water, peel, and let cool. Rinse dill tips and parsley leaves briefly in cold water and pat dry.

2 For the sushi, pat dry steelhead and halibut. Remove any bones with tweezers. Using a sharp knife, cut each fillet into six paper-thin slices of about 1½ in x 1½ in (4 x 4 cm). Trim frayed edges.

3 Remove yolk from hard-boiled egg and press through a fine-mesh strainer. Moisten your hands with vinegar water. Shape prepared sushi rice into 12 equal-sized balls.

4 For the steelhead trout temari, moisten a small kitchen towel or muslin cloth with vinegar water. Place 1 slice of fish in the center of the cloth and dab on wasabi paste with your fingertip. Place a rice ball on top. Grasp the ends of the cloth and twist them in opposite directions so that the rice and fish take on a spherical shape. Through the cloth, make a small depression in the center of the fish.

5 Remove steelhead temari from the cloth and arrange with the fish on top. Place 1 parsley leaf and a little egg yolk in the depression.

6 For the halibut temari, place 1 fish slice in the center of a damp cloth and dab on wasabi paste with your fingertip. Place 2 dill tips and 1 rice ball on top. Shape temari sushi as described above. Sprinkle a few chopped chives into the depression.

TIP—CLEVERLY SHAPED

Use an eggcup to make small temari sushi. Cut each fish fillet into 6 equal-sized slices. Brush an eggcup with oil and line with plastic wrap. Place 1 fish slice in the bottom of the cup, fill with rice and press down. Reverse egg cup onto a plate and carefully remove plastic wrap. Garnish the temari.

left: Steelhead Trout Temari | right: Halibut Temari

Pressed and Freestyle Sushi

These pressed sushi are always a hit! With one recipe, I can easily make 30 delicious morsels. Plus, they're pretty to look at. If I don't want plain fish, I can also have a topping of fish and vegetables or just vegetables.

Pressed Sea Bass and Steelhead Trout Sushi

5 oz (150 g) fresh skinless sea bass fillet
5 oz (150 g) fresh skinless steelhead trout fillet
Oil for the mold
1 recipe prepared sushi rice (page 8)
1 sheet toasted nori
1 scant tsp wasabi paste
Vinegar water
A rectangular mold (about 6 in x 8 in (15 x 21 cm))

Makes 30 sushi | ⊚ Prep time: 35 minutes
Per sushi approx.: 45 calories, 2 g protein,
1 g fat, 7 g carbohydrates

1 Pat both fish fillets dry and cut into thin strips
about 1 in (2–3 cm) wide. Brush oil into a rectangular mold (about 6 in x 8 in (15 x 21 cm)) and line
with plastic wrap.

2 For pressed sushi (see pages 36–37), place
alternating strips of sea bass and steelhead in the
bottom of the mold. Top with half the rice.

3 Brush one side of nori sheet with wasabi paste
and place on top of rice. Top with remaining rice,
smooth out the surface, and cover with plastic
wrap. Place a suitable lid on top and press down
evenly. Remove lid and top sheet of plastic wrap.

4 Carefully reverse pressed sushi onto a work
surface and remove plastic wrap. With a sharp
knife, cut into pieces about 1 in square (3 x 3 cm),
cleaning and moistening it with vinegar water after
each cut.

for company and parties

Pressed Marinated Sardine Sushi

If you're in a hurry, use commercially available marinated herring.
Drain fillets and pat dry.

9 oz (250 g) fresh sardine fillets with skin | 2 tbs sea salt | 7 tbs (100 ml) rice vinegar | 4 tsp mirin | 4 tsp sugar | Oil for the mold | 1 sheet toasted nori | 1 scant tsp wasabi paste | 1 recipe prepared sushi rice (page 8) | Vinegar water | A rectangular mold (about 6 in x 8 in (15 x 21 cm))

Makes 30 sushi | ⊕ Prep time: 35 minutes / Marinating time: 45 minutes
Per sushi approx.: 45 calories, 3 g protein, 1 g fat, 7 g carbohydrates

1 Rub salt into all sides of sardine fillets, wrap in plastic wrap, and refrigerate for 15 minutes. Rinse off salt under cold water and pat dry.

2 Layer fish fillets in a shallow bowl. Stir together rice vinegar, mirin, and sugar until sugar dissolves. Pour marinade over fish, cover, and marinate in the refrigerator for 30 minutes, turning once.

3 Remove fish from marinade and pat dry. With a sharp knife, cut an X several millimeters deep into the skin of each fillet (Figure 1).

4 Brush a thin layer of oil into a rectangular glass, porcelain, or plastic mold (about 6 in x 8 in (15 x 21 cm)) and line with plastic wrap. Cut nori sheet to fit the mold. Spread one side with a thin layer of wasabi paste. Pack bottom of mold with fish strips together, skin side down (Figure 2).

5 Dip a tablespoon into vinegar water and use it to distribute half the rice over the fish (Figure 3). Cover with a nori sheet with the wasabi side down (Figure 4).

6 Top with remaining rice, smooth out the surface, and cover with plastic wrap. Place a suitable lid or another mold on top of plastic wrap and press down evenly. Remove lid and top sheet of plastic wrap.

7 Carefully reverse sushi onto a work surface and remove plastic wrap. Moisten a sharp knife with vinegar water and cut sushi into pieces of about 1 in square (3 x 3 cm) (Figure 5), cleaning and moistening it with vinegar water after each cut. Serve with Japanese soy sauce, wasabi paste, and pickled ginger.

impressive

Pressed Striped Sushi

To be authentic, this should be accompanied by green tea. But it goes just as well with warm sake or a cold beer.

1 small red bell pepper | 1 small orange bell pepper | ½ ripe avocado | 2 tsp lemon juice | 7 oz (200 g) herb or smoked tofu | 1 sheet toasted nori | 1 scant tsp wasabi paste | Oil for the mold | 1 recipe prepared sushi rice (page 8) | About 30 herb leaves for garnish | Sea salt | Freshly ground pepper | Vinegar water | A rectangular mold (about 6 in x 8 in (15 x 21 cm))

Makes 30 sushi | ⏲ Prep time: 45 minutes
Per sushi approx.: 55 calories, 1 g protein,
2 g fat, 8 g carbohydrates

1 Preheat oven to 475°F (250°C). Rinse bell peppers, cut in half, and clean. Place in an oven-proof baking dish, skin side up. Bake in the oven for about 15 minutes until peel blisters and turns black. Let stand briefly.

2 Remove peel from peppers and cut into strips about ¾ in (2 cm) wide. Season lightly with salt and pepper. Peel avocado half, cut in half length-wise, and remove pit. Cut into slices ¼ in (½ cm) thick and then into strips about ¾ in (2 cm) wide. Drizzle immediately with lemon juice.

3 Cut tofu crosswise into slices ¼ in (½ cm) thick and 1–1½ in (3–4 cm) wide. Cut nori sheet to fit the mold and spread one side with a thin layer of wasabi paste.

4 Brush a thin layer of oil onto a rectangular glass, porcelain, or plastic mold (about 6 in x 8 in (15 x 21 cm)) and line with plastic wrap. Line bottom of the mold diagonally with alternating pieces of bell pepper and avocado, pressed tightly together.

5 Dip a tablespoon into vinegar water and use it to distribute half the rice in the mold and smooth out the surface. Cover with nori sheet, wasabi side down. Next, add a layer of tofu. Top with remaining rice, smooth out the surface, and cover with plastic wrap.

6 Place a suitable lid or another mold on top of plastic wrap and press down evenly. Remove lid and top sheet of plastic wrap.

7 Carefully reverse sushi onto a work surface and remove plastic wrap. Moisten a sharp knife with vinegar water and carefully cut sushi into pieces of about 1 in square (3 x 3 cm), cleaning and moistening it with vinegar water after each cut. Garnish sushi with herb leaves.

crossover

Italian-Style Hosomaki

I bet even the Japanese would love this "Italian" sushi.

1½ oz (40 g) dried tomatoes in oil | 2½ oz (80 g) mozzarella | 12 basil leaves | 2 sheets toasted nori | ½ recipe prepared sushi rice (page 8) | 4 tsp basil pesto (commercial product) | Vinegar water

Makes 24 sushi | ⊙ Prep time: 30 minutes
Per sushi approx.: 35 calories, 1 g protein,
1 g fat, 5 g carbohydrates

1 Drain tomatoes in a strainer. Cut lengthwise into strips ¼ in (½ cm) wide. Drain mozzarella and cut into slices ¼ in (½ cm) thick. Rinse basil, pat dry, and cut into strips.

2 Cut nori sheets in half crosswise. Using a rolling mat, make four maki rolls (see pages 12–13). Place half a nori sheet on mat, shiny side down and flush with the bottom. Moisten your hands with vinegar water. Distribute one-fourth of the sushi rice on the nori, leaving ¾ in (2 cm) uncovered at the two longer edges.

3 Make a lengthwise depression in the middle of the rice and spread 1 teaspoon pesto evenly inside. Top with one-fourth of the basil leaves, tomatoes, and mozzarella. Make into a firm maki roll and cut into six equal-sized pieces.

decorative | simply delicious

Asparagus Maki

From now on, you can add this to your list of "favorite snacks."

4 thick green asparagus spears | 3 tbs (50 ml) soy sauce | 3 tbs (50 ml) mirin | 2 tsp lemon juice | 2 tsp sugar | 4 large slices raw ham (e.g., smoked or Black Forest ham) | 2 sheets toasted nori | ½ recipe prepared sushi rice (page 8) | Vinegar water

Makes 24 sushi | ⊙ Prep time: 40 minutes
Per sushi approx.: 60 calories, 2 g protein,
3 g fat, 6 g carbohydrates

1 Rinse asparagus, cut off woody ends, and peel the bottom third. In a shallow pot, combine ½ cup (100 ml) water, soy sauce, mirin, lemon juice, and sugar and bring to a boil. Add asparagus, cover, and cook for 8–10 minutes until crisp-tender. Remove from water and drain.

2 Trim fat from ham. Cut nori sheets in half crosswise. Using a rolling mat, make four maki rolls (see pages 12–13). Place half a nori sheet on mat, shiny side down and flush with bottom. Moisten your hands with vinegar water. Distribute one-fourth of the sushi rice on the nori.

3 Place 1 ham slice on rice and spread a little wasabi paste down the center. Place an asparagus spear on top and make into a firm maki roll. Cut into six equal-sized pieces.

really easy and decorative

Vegetable Futomaki

Cheese ensures that each bite is fresh and creamy.

½ red bell pepper | ½ yellow bell pepper | 4 stalks celery | 4 radishes | 2 tsp olive oil | 2½ oz (80 g) soft herb cheese (such as herbed Boursin, Alouette, Rondelé, cream cheese, goat cheese, or yogurt cheese) | 2 sheets toasted nori | ½ recipe prepared sushi rice (page 8) | Sea salt | Freshly ground pepper | Vinegar water

Makes 16 sushi | Prep time: 30 minutes
Per sushi approx.: 50 calories, 2 g protein, 1 g fat, 8 g carbohydrates

1 Rinse and clean vegetables. Cut bell peppers and celery lengthwise into strips ¼ in (½ cm) wide. Cut radishes into matchsticks or grate coarsely. Toss vegetables with oil and season with salt and pepper. Stir cheese until smooth.

2 Using a rolling mat, make two thick maki sushi (see pages 12–13). Place 1 whole nori sheet on the mat, shiny side down and flush with bottom. Moisten your hands with vinegar water. Distribute half the sushi rice on the nori, leaving a margin uncovered at the top and bottom.

3 Arrange half vegetables and cheese lengthwise along the lower third of rice. Make into a thick roll. Use remaining ingredients to make a second roll. Moisten a sharp knife with vinegar water and cut futomaki rolls into eight equal-sized pieces.

unusual

Herring Futomaki

Herring and apple—in this sushi, they're a kickin' combo!

5 oz (150 g) Matjes herring fillets | 1 red apple ½ tbs lemon juice | 2 green onions | 2 sheets toasted nori | ½ recipe prepared sushi rice (page 8) | ½ tbs horseradish cream

Makes 16 sushi | Prep time: 30 minutes
Per sushi approx.: 65 calories, 2 g protein, 8 g fat, 2 g carbohydrates

1 Pat herring dry and cut lengthwise into strips ¼ in (½ cm) thick. Rinse apple, dry, cut in half, and remove core. Cut apple into matchsticks ¼ in (½ cm) thick and immediately drizzle with lemon juice. Rinse green onions and clean, removing the white part.

2 Make two thick maki sushi (see pages 12–13). For each roll, use 1 nori sheet, half prepared rice, cream horseradish, green part of green onions, and apple matchsticks. Cut futomaki into eight equal-sized pieces. Arrange on a plate and serve.

PLUS
This sushi is excellent with cold beer, whether light or Pilsner.

Three Sushi Canapés

Another new form of sushi shape, and super-fast as well — cut them out, add a topping, and they're done!

1 small carrot | 1 tsp grated coconut | 1 tsp oil | 4 quail eggs | 8 Italian parsley leaves | 1 green onion | 2 oz (50 g) fresh tuna or salmon fillet | 1 recipe prepared sushi rice (page 8) | Black or white sesame seeds | 2 tbs mixed, finely chopped herbs | Sea salt | Cayenne pepper | Vinegar water | Cookie cutter (about 1½ in (4 cm) diameter)

Makes 24 sushi | ⊚ Prep time: 45 minutes
Per sushi approx.: 60 calories, 2 g protein,
2 g fat, 9 g carbohydrates

1   For Chili Carrot Canapés, peel carrots, clean, and dice finely. In an ungreased pan, toast coconut until golden-brown, then remove. Add oil to pan, heat, and braise carrots for 5-7 minutes until crisp-tender. Drain in a strainer. Add coconut and season with salt and a little cayenne pepper.

2   For Quail Egg Canapés, boil eggs for 4 minutes. Plunge into cold water, let cool, peel, cut in half lengthwise, and salt lightly. Rinse parsley leaves and pat dry.

3   For Fish Tartare Canapés, rinse green onions, clean, and pat dry. Chop onions and fish very finely. Season with 1 pinch salt.

4   Spread a ½ in to ¾ in (1½ to 2 cm) thick layer of sushi rice on a work surface. With a cookie cutter, cut out 24 disks, constantly dipping the cutter in vinegar water.

5   Roll eight disks in sesame seeds around their circumference and top with 1 parsley leaf and 1 egg half. Roll eight in herbs and top with chili carrots. Place a little fish tartare on the center of the remaining eight.

left: Chili Carrot Canapés | middle: Fish Tartare Canapés | right: Quail Egg Canapés

Roast Beef Nigiri

8 slices roast beef | 16 small Italian parsley leaves | 3 equal-sized mushrooms | 1 tsp lemon juice | 2 tsp remoulade sauce | ½ recipe prepared sushi rice (page 8) | Vinegar water

Makes 8 sushi | ⏲ Prep time: 30 minutes
Per sushi approx.: 200 calories, 24 g protein, 5 g fat, 13 g carbohydrates

1   From the center of the roast beef, cut out a 1 x 2 in (3 x 5 cm) piece. Rinse parsley and pat dry. Wipe mushrooms, remove stems, slice caps, and drizzle immediately with lemon juice.

2   Spread a thin layer of remoulade sauce on one side of each piece of roast beef. Moisten your hands with vinegar water. Shape sushi rice into eight rectangular blocks. Make nigiri sushi using roast beef and rice (see pages 24–25). Garnish with mushroom slices and parsley leaves.

Parma Ham Nigiri

8–16 long chive leaves | 8 slices Parma ham | 4 walnuts | 4 pitted black olives | 1 tsp tomato paste | ½ recipe prepared sushi rice (page 8) | Vinegar water

Makes 8 sushi | ⏲ Prep time: 35 minutes
Per sushi approx.: 175 calories, 9 g protein, 10 g fat, 14 g carbohydrates

1   Rinse chives and pat dry. From the center of the Parma ham slices, cut out a 1 x 2 in (3 x 5 cm) piece. Finely chop walnuts and olives. Toss both gently with sushi rice.

2   Spread a thin layer of tomato paste on one side of each piece of ham. Moisten your hands with vinegar water. Shape sushi rice into eight rectangular blocks. Make nigiri sushi from Parma ham and rice (see pages 24–25). Knot 1–2 chives around each one.

fancy

Duck Temaki

These sushi cones are a delight, with their delicate, sharply contrasting interiors.

7 oz (200 g) duck breast fillet | 1 tbs pink pepper-corns | 2 tsp oil | 5 oz (150 g) mango flesh | 12 sprigs cilantro (may substitute Italian parsley) | 3 sheets toasted nori | ½ recipe prepared sushi rice (page 8) | Sea salt | Vinegar water

Makes 6 sushi | ⊚ Prep time: 40 minutes
Per sushi approx.: 190 calories, 8 g protein, 8 g fat, 21 g carbohydrates

1   Pat dry duck breast. Crush pepper coarsely. In a pan, heat oil until very hot and fry duck 2–4 minutes on each side. Remove from pan and dab off fat. Season duck with salt and pepper and slice thinly against the grain

2   Cut mango lengthwise into strips ¼ in (½ cm) wide. Rinse cilantro and pat dry. Cut nori sheets in half crosswise.

3   Moisten your hands with vinegar water. Shape rice into six equal-sized balls. Roll temaki into cones using ½ sheet nori, one rice ball, and one-sixth of the duck breast, mango, and cilantro (see page 28). Seal the outside edge of the nori with a couple mashed grains of rice.

juicy | spicy

Chicken Temaki

Honestly, have you ever eaten such a fantastic chicken snack?

5 oz (150 g) skinless chicken breast fillet | 1 piece fresh ginger (1¼ in (3 cm)) | 1 clove garlic | 2 tsp light soy sauce | 1 small carrot | 1 bunch chives or garlic chives | 3 sheets toasted nori | ½ recipe prepared sushi rice (page 8) | 4 tsp sweet-and-sour chili sauce | Vinegar water

Makes 6 sushi | ⊚ Prep time: 40 minutes
Per sushi approx.: 115 calories, 8 g protein, 1 g fat, 19 g carbohydrates

1   Place chicken in a small pot and add just enough water to cover. Peel ginger and garlic and slice. Add ginger, garlic, and soy sauce to the pot. Bring to a boil, cover, and simmer gently for 10 minutes. Remove chicken from water and pat dry. Let cool slightly and cut into strips.

2   Rinse carrot and peel. First cut lengthwise into thin slices and then into very fine strips. Rinse chives and pat dry. Cut nori sheets in half crosswise.

3   Moisten your hands with vinegar water. Shape rice into six equal-sized balls. Roll temaki into cones using ½ sheet nori, one rice ball, ⅔ teaspoon chili sauce and one-sixth of the chicken, carrot, and chives (see page 28).

left: Duck Temaki | right: Chicken Temaki

Sushi Sides

It's wonderful when the spicy sesame essence of spinach salad spreads over your tongue. For me, this is an integral part of a successful sushi meal. There can also be soup or a skewer, but it is not complete without this salad.

Spinach Salad with Sesame Seed Dressing

1 lb 2 oz (500 g) fresh spinach
2 tsp sesame seeds
2 tsp sesame paste (1 oz (30 g), substitute tahini)
4 tsp light soy sauce
2 tbs dashi (instant fish stock) or water
¼ tsp sugar (or more to taste)
Kosher salt

Serves 4 | ⊙ Prep time: 30 minutes
Per serving approx.: 65 calories, 4 g protein,
4 g fat, 4 g carbohydrates

1 Rinse spinach in cold standing water. Drain and remove stems. Bring salted water to a boil and blanch spinach for 1 minute. Pour off water, plunge into ice-cold water, and drain well. Squeeze out spinach and pull apart.

2 In an ungreased pan, toast sesame seeds. For the dressing, combine sesame paste, soy sauce, dashi or water, and sugar and mix until smooth and creamy.

3 Toss spinach with dressing and salt to taste. Transfer to four small dishes and serve sprinkled with toasted sesame seeds.

VARIATION—BEANS WITH SESAME SEED DRESSING
Cook 11 oz (300 g) frozen green beans in boiling salted water for about 5 minutes. Plunge into ice-cold water and drain well. Prepare sesame seed dressing as described above. Combine beans and dressing and salt to taste. Serve sprinkled with 2 teaspoons toasted sesame seeds.

Vegetables with Teriyaki Dip

6 tbs teriyaki sauce | ½ tspgrated ginger | ¼ tsp red chili paste (sambal oelek) | 1 tbs cilantro or basil leaves | 1 small endive | 1 zucchini | 1 carrot | 4 stalks celery

Serves 4 | 🕐 Prep time: 25 minutes
Per serving approx.: 70 calories, 5 g protein, 1 g fat, 12 g carbohydrates

1   For dip, combine teriyaki sauce, ginger, and chili paste. Rinse herb leaves, pat dry, chop finely, and add to dip. Transfer to a deep bowl.

2   Separate endive leaves. Cut zucchini, carrot, and celery into long strips. Arrange vegetables in tall glasses and serve with teriyaki dip.

Radish Carrot Salad

7 oz (200 g) daikon radish | 7 oz (200 g) carrots | 2 tsp salt | 2 tsp lemon zest | 3 tbs rice vinegar | ½ tsp sugar | 4 tsp light soy sauce | ½ tsp freshly grated ginger

Serves 4 | 🕐 Prep time: 30 minutes |
Marinating time: 1 hour and 10 minutes
Per serving approx.: 33 calories, 1 g protein, 1 g fat, 6 g carbohydrates

1   Rinse radish and carrots, peel, and slice into matchsticks 1½ in (4 cm) long. Mix with salt and let stand for 10 minutes. Rinse under cold running water, drain, and pat dry.

2   Combine lemon zest, vinegar, sugar, soy sauce, and ginger and stir until sugar dissolves. Pour over vegetables and marinate for 1 hour, stirring occasionally.

Chinese Cabbage Rolls

16 Chinese cabbage leaves (about 11 oz (300 g)) |
7 oz (200 ml) rice vinegar | 2 tsp salt | 2 tsp honey
| 4 tsp light soy sauce | 2 tsp grated ginger |
½ tsp hot paprika | 1 bunch chives

Serves 4 | ⊚ Prep time: 25 minutes |
Marinating time: 12 hours
Per serving approx.: 45 calories, 2 g protein,
1 g fat, 10 g carbohydrates

1   Rinse cabbage leaves, drain, and layer in a shallow bowl. Boil vinegar, salt, and honey. Stir in soy
sauce, ginger, and paprika. Pour over cabbage, cover with plastic wrap, and place a weight on top.
Marinate in the refrigerator for at least 12 hours.

2   To serve, thoroughly drain cabbage in a strainer
and roll up each leaf tightly. Knot a chive around
each leaf to secure.

Sprout Salad

7 oz (200 g) bean sprouts | 1 carrot | 1 small red
bell pepper | 2 tsp canola oil | 1 scant tsp dark
sesame oil | 4–6 tsp light soy sauce | 4 tsp rice
vinegar | Kosher salt

Serves 4 | ⊚ Prep time: 25 minutes
Per serving approx.: 80 calories, 4 g protein,
5 g fat, 6 g carbohydrates

1   Sort sprouts. Rinse carrot and bell pepper, and
cut into matchsticks 1½–2 in (4–5 cm) long. For the
dressing, beat together canola oil, sesame oil, and
soy sauce.

2   Bring salted water to a boil and blanch carrot for
1 minute. Add sprouts and bell pepper and briefly
return to a boil. Pour off water, plunge into cold
water, and drain thoroughly. Toss vegetables with
dressing and serve immediately.

Chicken and Glass Noodle Soup

The ideal culinary addition when you don't want to fill yourself up on sushi alone.

5 oz (150 g) skinless chicken breast fillet |
1 scant tsp sake | 4 tsp light soy sauce | 1½ oz
(40 g) glass noodles | 3 oz (100 g) snow peas |
8 small cherry tomatoes | 3¼ cups (800 ml)
dashi (instant fish stock) | Kosher salt | Shichimi
togarashi (hot spice mixture)

Serves 4 | Prep time: 30 minutes
Per serving approx.: 175 calories, 16 g protein,
6 g fat, 20 g carbohydrates

1   Pat dry chicken breast and slice thinly. Toss with
sake and 2 teaspoons soy sauce and marinate
briefly. Place noodles in a bowl and pour hot water
over the top. Let soak for 10 minutes

2   Rinse snow peas, clean, and cut into pieces on
an angle. Bring salted water to a bowl and blanch
peas for 2 minutes. Plunge into ice-cold water
and drain.

3   Rinse cherry tomatoes and cut in half crosswise.
Bring dashi to a boil and simmer chicken over low
heat for 3 minutes.

4   Drain noodles in a strainer and cut up with
scissors. Add noodles, peas, and tomatoes to soup
and simmer for 5 minutes but do not boil. Add
2 teaspoons soy sauce, salt, and a little shichimi
togarashi to taste.

VARIATION—SHRIMP SOUP
Instead of chicken, use 4 raw shrimp. Peel shrimp, score
along the backs, and devein. Rinse shrimp, pat dry,
marinate, and cook for 2 minutes. Prepare soup as
described above. Season with lime zest and leave out
the shichimi togarashi.

Egg Drop Soup

1 small carrot | 3¼ cups (800 ml) hearty
chicken stock (preferably homemade) | 2 eggs |
2 tsp mirin | 4 tsp light soy sauce | 1 tsp lemon
juice | Kosher salt

Serves 4 | ⊚ Prep time: 20 minutes
Per serving approx.: 110 calories, 14 g protein,
5 g fat, 2 g carbohydrates

1 Rinse carrot, peel, and cut into slices ¼ in
(½ cm) thick (if desired, cut into flower shapes
using a cutter). Bring stock to a boil and simmer
carrots for 6–8 minutes until crisp-tender.

2 Beat eggs, stopping before they become foamy.
Remove stock from heat and drizzle eggs into stock
while stirring. Season to taste with mirin, soy sauce,
lemon juice, and salt.

Tofu Miso Soup

1 thin leek | 4 shiitake mushrooms | 3¼ cups
(800 ml) dashi (instant fish stock) | 7 oz (200 g)
firm tofu | 2½ oz (80 g) red miso paste (soy bean
paste) | 4 tsp mirin | Kosher salt | Cilantro leaves
for garnish

Serves 4 | ⊚ Prep time: 20 minutes
Per serving approx.: 190 calories, 7 g protein,
9 g fat, 12 g carbohydrates

1 Clean leek, rinse, and slice very thinly. Wipe
mushrooms, remove stems, and cut caps into quarters. Bring dashi to a boil and simmer leek and
mushrooms for 3 minutes.

2 Cut tofu into equal-sized cubes. Stir miso
paste into a little stock. Add to remaining stock,
which is no longer boiling, and stir until smooth.
Add tofu and let stand for 4 minutes. Season to
taste with mirin and salt and serve garnished
with cilantro leaves.

enjoy very fresh

Vegetable Shrimp Tempura

Dip into a world of smiles: Vegetables and shrimp surrounded by a crispy batter served with a spicy sauce.

For the tempura
2 carrots | 1 zucchini | 1 small eggplant | 1 bunch green onions | 8 fresh shiitake or white mushrooms | 8 small raw shrimp (about 5 oz (150 g)) | 4 cups (1 liter) oil for frying

For the dip
4 tbs Japanese soy sauce | 4 tbs mirin | 2 tbs sake | 1 piece radish (about 1½ in (4 cm)) | 1 piece fresh ginger (about 1¼ in (3 cm))

For the batter
1 egg | ½ cup (125 g) flour + flour for dredging

Serves 4 | ⓘ Prep time: 55 minutes
Per serving approx.: 380 calories, 17 g protein, 16 g fat, 34 g carbohydrates

1   Rinse vegetables, pat dry, and peel. Cut carrots, zucchini, and eggplant on an angle into slices ¼ in (½ cm) thick. Cut green onions into pieces 1¼ in (3 cm) long. Clean mushrooms.

2   Peel shrimp, score along the backs, and devein. Rinse shrimp and pat dry. Refrigerate vegetables and shrimp.

3   For the dip, briefly bring mirin and sake to a boil and let cool. Peel radish and ginger, grate finely, and stir into dip. Transfer to four small dishes.

4   For the batter, beat together 7 fluid oz (200 ml) ice-cold water and egg and quickly beat in flour. In a wok or pot, heat oil. Preheat oven to 150°F (70°C).

5   First dredge vegetables and shrimp in flour. Then dip into batter in batches and deep-fry in hot oil for 1–2 minutes until slightly golden and crispy.

6   With a skimmer, remove tempura from oil and drain on paper towels. Keep warm in the oven until all ingredients are fried and crispy. Serve tempura with dip (and chopsticks).

TIP FOR SUCCESS
For good tempura, the most important thing is that you use ice-cold water for the batter and stir it only very briefly. Don't worry if a few small lumps of flour remain.

VARIATION—FISH TEMPURA
Cut up 14 oz (400 g) of any type of fish fillet. Peel 1 small sweet potato (may substitute a firm potato) and slice thinly. Rinse 1 red bell pepper, clean, and cut into strips. Prepare as described in the recipe above. If desired, add fish and shrimp.

for special occasions

Beef Tenderloin Skewers

Extremely easy to prepare and simply tip-top!

9 oz (250 g) marbled beef tenderloin (trimmed) | 4 tsp mirin | ½ tsp sugar | 2 tbs light soy sauce | Japanese sansho pepper (may substitute black pepper) | 1 bunch green onions | 2 tbs oil for frying | 8 wooden skewers

Serves 4 | Prep time: 30 minutes | Marinating time: 4 hours
Per serving approx.: 190 calories, 15 g protein, 12 g fat, 4 g carbohydrates

1 Cut beef tenderloin into 16 equal-sized cubes. Stir together mirin, sugar, and soy sauce until the sugar dissolves. Season marinade with pepper. Add beef, cover, and marinate in the refrigerator for 4 hours.

2 Rinse green onions, clean, and cut white and light-green parts into pieces 1¼–1½ in (3–4 cm) long (a total of 24 pieces). Remove meat from marinade and drain. Alternately thread three onion pieces and two meat cubes onto each skewer.

3 In a large pan, heat oil and fry skewers in batches on all sides for 3–4 minutes while brushing on remaining marinade. Beef Tenderloin Skewers are delicious hot or cold.

super simple

Chicken Yakitori

These skewers have a large following in Japan.

½ cup (125 ml) mirin (may substitute semi-dry white wine) | 2 tsp sugar | ¼ cup (75 ml) Japanese soy sauce | 12 oz (350 g) skinless chicken breast fillet | 2 small red bell peppers | 4 lime wedges | 8 wooden skewers

Serves 4 | Prep time: 30 minutes
Per serving approx.: 150 calories, 22 g protein, 1 g fat, 8 g carbohydrates

1 For marinade, bring mirin and sugar to a boil. Stir in soy sauce, return to a boil, and let cool slightly.

2 Pat dry chicken breast and cut into 24 equal-sized pieces. Rinse bell peppers, and cut into 16 equal-sized pieces. Alternately thread 3 chicken pieces and 2–3 bell pepper cubes onto each skewer.

3 Place skewers side by side in a shallow bowl. Pour marinade over the top, turn skewers, and marinate for 10 minutes.

4 Heat oven broiler. Remove skewers from marinade, drain, and place side by side on a rack covered with aluminum foil. Broil for 3 minutes. Then turn and broil for another 3–4 minutes, repeatedly brushing with marinade until they appear glazed. Serve Chicken Yakitori with lime wedges.

left: Chicken Yakitori | right: Beef Tenderloin Skewer

slightly exotic | not too sweet

Coconut-Lime Ice Cream

*Especially delicious, just right for
closing a meal.*

1 cup (250 ml) coconut milk | ¼ cup (60 g) sugar |
1 tbs Bourbon vanilla | 1 lime | 5 oz (150 g)
sour cream

Serves 4 | ⊚ Prep time: 20 minutes |
Freezing time: 45 minutes
Per serving approx.: 250 calories, 2 g protein,
17 g fat, 22 g carbohydrates

1 Combine coconut milk, sugar, and vanilla and
bring to a boil while stirring. Remove from heat and
let cool until lukewarm.

2 Rinse lime under hot water and wipe dry. Grate
peel finely. Squeeze juice from ½ lime. Stir lime
peel and sour cream into the coconut milk mixture.
Season to taste with lime juice

3 Pour mixture into an ice cream maker and freeze
for 30–45 minutes. (If you don't have an ice cream
maker, freeze the mixture in a shallow metal bowl
for about 3 hours, occasionally stirring well with a
wire whisk to make the ice cream creamy.) Scoop
out Coconut-Lime Ice Cream and serve.

VARIATION WITH CARAMELIZED PINEAPPLE
Serve ice cream with caramelized pineapple. In a pan,
heat 1 tablespoon butter until frothy. Sprinkle in 2 tablespoons sugar and melt until golden brown. Add about
11 oz (300 g) fresh pineapple pieces and toss. Serve
warm with ice cream.

slightly chilled, it's a masterpiece

Tropical Fruit Salad

*Fine, fruity, and refreshing—
a high-class dessert!*

1 piece ginger (¾ in (2 cm)) | 1 lime | 1 tsp honey |
6 mint leaves | 1 ripe mango | 1 ripe papaya |
1 baby pineapple

Serves 4 | ⊚ Prep time: 30 minutes
Per serving approx.: 110 calories, 1 g protein,
1 g fat, 26 g carbohydrates

1 Peel ginger and grate finely. Rinse lime with
hot water and wipe dry. Finely grate 1 teaspoon
peel and squeeze out lime juice. Combine
2 tablespoons lime juice, grated lime peel, ginger,
and honey, and stir until smooth. Rinse mint leaves
and cut two into fine strips.

2 Peel mango and cut fruit from the pit in wide
strips. Cut papaya in half lengthwise and remove
seeds with a spoon. Peel papaya halves. Peel
pineapple and cut into quarters. Cut all fruit into
bite-sized, decorative pieces.

3 Immediately add lime-ginger mixture and mint
strips to fruit. Season to taste with lime juice. Cover
and refrigerate. Serve garnished with remaining
mint leaves.

top: Coconut-Lime Ice Cream | bottom: Tropical Fruit Salad

Using this Index

To help you find recipes containing certain ingredients even more quickly, this index also lists favorite ingredients (such as shrimp and mushrooms) in alphabetical order and bold type, followed by the corresponding recipes.

A

Apples: herring futomaki 42
Arugula: mushroom and arugula futomaki 16
Asparagus maki 40
Avocado: crispy salmon and avocado hosomaki 12

B

Beef tenderloin skewers 56
Beef
  beef tenderloin skewers 56
  steak temaki 30

C

California roll: surimi uramaki 18
Canapés: three sushi canapés 44
Carrots
  egg drop soup 53
  carrot and zucchini hosomaki 14
  chili carrot canapés: three sushi canapés 44
  radish carrot salad 50
  vegetable shrimp tempura 54
  vegetables with teriyaki dip 50
Caviar
  roe gunkan-maki (variation) 20
  salmon and roe nigiri 22
Celery: vegetables with teriyaki dip 50
Chicken
  chicken and glass noodle soup 52
  chicken temaki 46
  chicken yakitori 56
Chili carrots: three sushi canapés 44

Chinese cabbage rolls 51
Coconut-lime ice cream 58

D

Dashi—see instant dashi (ingredients) 6
Drinks (know-how) 5
Duck: duck temaki 46

E

Eggplant: vegetable shrimp tempura 54
Eggs
  egg drop soup 53
  omelet nigiri (variation) 26
  quail eggs: three sushi canapés 44
  scrambled egg gunkan-maki (variation) 20
Endive: vegetables with teriyaki dip 50

F

Fish
  fish tartare: three sushi canapés 44
  fish tempura (variation) 54
  raw fish (know-how) 4
Fruit salad: tropical fruit salad 58
Futomaki
  herring futomaki 42
  mushroom and arugula futomaki 16
  squash futomaki (variation) 16
  trout futomaki (variation) 16
  vegetable futomaki 42

G

Gari-shoga—pickled ginger (ingredients) 6
Ginger: pickled ginger (ingredients) 6
Glass noodles: chicken and glass noodle soup 52
Gravlax: gravlax temaki 28

Gunkan-maki
  roe gunkan-maki (variation) 20
  scrambled egg gunkan-maki (variation) 20
  shrimp salad gunkan-maki 20

H

Halibut: two types of temari sushi 32
Ham: asparagus maki 40
Herring futomaki 42
Horseradish—see wasabi (ingredients) 6
Hosomaki
  carrot and zucchini hosomaki 14
  crispy salmon and avocado hosomaki 12
  Italian-style hosomaki 40
  marinated tuna hosomaki 10

I

Ice cream: coconut-lime ice cream 58
Instant dashi (ingredients) 6
Iodine (useful information) 64

J

Japanese soy sauce (ingredients) 6

L

Limes: coconut-lime ice cream 58

M

Mackerel: marinated mackerel nigiri 26
Maki: asparagus maki 40
Mango: tropical fruit salad 58
Measurement guide (know-how) 5
Mirin (ingredients) 6
Mozzarella: Italian-style hosomaki 40
Mushrooms
  mushroom and arugula futomaki 16
  mushroom temaki 30

N

Nigiri
    marinated mackerel nigiri 26
    omelet nigiri (variation) 26
    Parma ham nigiri 45
    roast beef nigiri 45
    salmon and roe nigiri 22
    shrimp nigiri (variation) 26
    tuna nigiri 24
Nori sheets (ingredients) 6

O

Omelet nigiri (variation) 26
Oyster mushrooms: mushroom
    temaki 30

P

Papaya: tropical fruit salad 58
Parma ham nigiri 45
Pickled ginger (ingredients) 6
Pineapple: exotic fruit salad 58
Pressed marinated sardine sushi 36
Pressed sea bass and steelhead
    sushi 34
Pressed striped sushi 38

Q

Quail eggs: three sushi canapés 44

R

Radish carrot salad 50
Rice vinegar (ingredients) 6
Rice wine—mirin (ingredients) 6
Roast beef nigiri 45

S

Salads
    radish carrot salad 50
    sprout salad 51
    tropical fruit salad 58
Salmon
    crispy salmon and avocado
        hosomaki 12
    fish tartare, three sushi
        canapés 44

    gravlax temaki 28
    salmon and roe nigiri 22
Sardines: pressed marinated
    sardine sushi 36
Sea bass: pressed sea bass and
    steelhead sushi 36
Sesame oil (ingredients) 6
Shiitake mushrooms
    tofu miso soup 53
    vegetable shrimp tempura 54
Shoyu—see Japanese soy sauce
    (ingredients) 6
Shrimp salad gunkan-maki 20
Shrimp soup (variation) 52
Shrimp
    shrimp nigiri (variation) 26
    Shrimp soup (variation) 52
    vegetable shrimp tempura 54
Snow peas: chicken and glass
    noodle soup 14
Soy sauce (ingredients) 6
Spinach salad with sesame
    seed dressing 48
Sprout salad 51
Squash futomaki (variation) 16
Steak temaki 30
Steelhead
    pressed sea bass and steelhead
        trout sushi 34
    two types of temari sushi 32
Su—rice vinegar (ingredients) 6
Surimi uramaki 18
Sushi rice (basic recipe) 8
Sushi rice (ingredients) 6

T

Temaki
    chicken 46
    duck temaki 46
    gravlax temaki 28
    mushroom temaki 30
    steak temaki 30
    tofu temaki 28
Temari sushi: two types of temari
    sushi 32

Tempura
    fish tempura (variation) 54
    vegetable shrimp tempura 54
Teriyaki dip: vegetables with teriyaki
    dip 50
Three sushi canapés 44
Tofu
    tofu miso soup 53
    tofu temaki 28
Tropical fruit salad 58
Trout futomaki (variation) 16
Tuna
    marinated tuna hosomaki 10
    three sushi canapés 44
    tuna nigiri 24
    tuna uramaki (variation) 18
Two types of temari sushi 32

U

Uramaki
    surimi uramaki 18
    tuna uramaki (variation) 18

V

Vegetable:
    futomaki 42
    shrimp tempura 54
Vegetables with teriyaki dip 50
Vinegar water (know-how) 4

W

Wasabi (ingredients) 6

Z

Zucchini: carrot and zucchini
    hosomaki 14

Thank you!
A special thanks to Bamboo Garden for providing the sushi accessories in this book.

Published originally under the title Sushi © 2006 Gräfe und Unzer Verlag GmbH, Munich. English translation for the U.S. market © 2007, Silverback Books, Inc.

Program director: Doris Birk
Managing editor: Birgit Rademacker, Lynda Zuber Sassi
Editor: Monika Greiner, Ann Beman
Reader: Katharina Lisson
Translation: Christie Tam
Layout, typography, and cover design: Independent Medien-Design, Munich
Typesetting: Liebl Satz+Grafik, Emmering
Production: Martina Müller, Patty Holden

Printed in China

ISBN-10: 1-59637-234-6
ISBN-13: 978-1-59637-234-4

The Author

Marlisa Szwillus is a culinary journalist, nutrition scientist, and author of more than 30 books. For several years, she managed the cooking department of the largest German food magazine. As an Asiaphile with experience in Far-Eastern culinary arts, she gives these recipes a creative and modern touch that makes them easy to follow, even for us Westerners.

The Photographers

For years, the **L'EVEQUE Tanja & Harry Bischof** (Food & Styling) Studio in Munich has been working for advertisers, books, and magazines in the food industry. In Munich the team creates food photos that demonstrate refreshing and trendy styling. The ceramic products are courtesy of Eva Frohwein.

Photo Credits

Cover photo: Joerg Lehmann, Paris. All other photos: Tanja & Harry Bischof, Munich

Cover Recipe

Bottom: 3 Carrot and Zucchini Hosomaki from page 14. Top: 1 Salmon and Roe Nigiri from page 22.

Enjoy these Quick & Easy Books in their new format

Antipasti and Tapas

MARTIN KINTRUP

SILVERBACK

Fondue

CLAUDIA LENZ

SILVERBACK

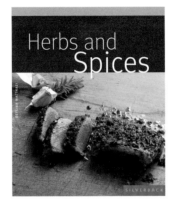

Herbs and Spices

BETTINA MATTHAEI

SILVERBACK

Raclette

CORNELIA SCHINHARL

SILVERBACK

Salad

TANIA DUSY

SILVERBACK

Sushi

MARLISA SZWILLUS

SILVERBACK

Waffles

KRISTIANE MÜLLER-URBAN

SILVERBACK

Everything Else You Need to Know

Decorative and colorful

In Japan, arranging and serving sushi is an art in itself, with strict rules that must be followed. In your own home, you can be a little more relaxed and develop an individual aesthetic style. Nevertheless, it's good to know, for example, that nigiri and gunkan sushi are traditionally served to guests only in pairs, never alone or in threes. Also, a larger assortment of sushi should be as colorful as possible: red (tuna), white (sea bass or monkfish), blue (mackerel and sardines), orange (salmon), and yellow (omelet).

Host a Do-It-Yourself Party

Here's how: Put everything needed for the various types of sushi on a large table, including lots of nori sheets, lettuce leaves, sushi rice, and a range of ingredients for all sorts of toppings and fillings. Don't forget wasabi paste, as well as vinegar water. Guests can prepare their own sushi according to their hearts' desires. The fun starts before the actual meal. And here's another tip for making temaki sushi: Half a nori sheet rolls up to the size of an ice cream cone. A quarter of a nori sheet makes temaki proportionately smaller so people can try out a wider variety of fillings.

It's Good for You and Can Help You Get in Shape

Nutrition experts praise sushi as a balanced and extremely healthy food, because it's tremendously rich in nutrients while extremely low in fat. Fish and seafood supply the full range of nutrients and vital substances to promote mental and physical fitness, in particular high-quality and easily digestible protein, vitamins, minerals, and omega-3 fatty acids, which are so good for the cardiovascular system. Rice and vegetables contribute important carbohydrates and fiber. Nori sheets made from pressed seaweed are loaded with vitamins and minerals, especially iodine and vitamin B12.